I Want to Draw Closer to God,

A Guide to Help People Find a Relationship
with God

Kerry W. Williams

Waterford Church of Christ
4991 Williams Lake Rd.
Waterford, MI 48329
(248 674-1553

ISBN 978-1-938335-78-5

Special thanks are extended to Randy Simpkins, Julia Bristow, and Reagan Williams. Your advice was invaluable to the production of this material.

Foreword

I talk to people every day about God, Jesus, church, and religion. Some of these sweet people are involved with a church family while others are not. Some have very satisfying lives, while others are struggling every day to survive, either physically, financially, or emotionally. Yet most people share one distinct characteristic which binds them together in the brotherhood of humanity. The common trait most share is, when asked, the desire to draw closer to God.

Why do we share this desire to be more intimate with our Creator? When we look back through history at ancient cultures, they all shared one common trait: worship. Some worshipped the sun, carved stone, or nature itself; yet they all felt the *need* to worship. Why? I suppose the answer is that we all have an innate desire born within us. We need God.

Despite this desire, *wanting* to draw close to God and actually *following through with it* are two very different things. Where does a person begin? Do I go to church? Which church do I go to, and how can I tell if it's the right one for me? Do I read the Bible? If so, should I begin in the Old Testament or the New? Do I pray? What do I pray about? There are so many questions that often, people simply get frustrated and end up doing nothing at all. They want to build a relationship with God, but have absolutely no idea where to begin.

Although religion and faith can be intimidating, especially when a person is either just getting started or coming back to God, it is actually a very simple process. God wants to be close to you. He desires to have a relationship with you, and has revealed Himself to you in the Bible. All it takes is a willingness to follow His instructions, much like one would follow a map to lead him or her to a specific destination. In this case, the destination is a close and meaningful relationship with God, and the roadmap containing all the instructions needed is the Bible.

The Bible is a big book. Do we start in Genesis or Matthew? The answers we need are found throughout the pages of the Good Book, but finding those instructions can be challenging without help. The Bible is filled with marvelous but often confusing words and images. These images can be difficult to interpret and understand.

Therefore, we come to the purpose of this little book. It does not claim to have the answers you need in order to draw closer to God. It simply directs you to the Bible, so that you might find the answers there. God desires that you draw close to Him, and deep down inside, you desire to do the same.

What a glorious hope. You CAN have a relationship with God. But will you? If you so desire, turn the page and prepare to let God speak to you through His Word.

Step 1

Understanding the Problem

If God longs to have a relationship with man, and the need for God is built within everyone, then where is the problem? Why do so many well-meaning people live out their lives without God's presence? Why does it seem so very hard and confusing to have a relationship with Him?

The answer has to do with a simple, well-known, but seldom understood religious word: *sin*. If we were to ask, "What is sin?" people would likely respond, "Really bad stuff." In part, they would be right, but sin is much more than just the really repulsive things like murder and violence. It actually applies to a *principle* as much as it does to specific actions.

"All unrighteousness is sin…"[1]

"Whoever commits sin also commits lawlessness, and sin is lawlessness."[2]

---

[1] 1 John 5:17
[2] 1 John 3:4

These verses show us the very essence of what sin is. It is much more than simply telling a lie or stealing: it is a *concept* of right and wrong. Sin is the breaking of God's divine will. It is the violation of His holy desires. In essence, it is anything which contradicts what God wants!

That is why there are both *sins of commission* and *sins of omission*. "Commission" refers to those things we do which are wrong, while "omission" describes the *lack* of doing right. Both go against God's desire for our lives. He is our maker, and has a design for our existence. Sin occurs when we alter that supreme design.

Therefore, to live without sin would be to live one's life in complete harmony with God's will. Jesus did so. Everything He did and everything He said while on this earth were pleasing to God. That is why the Bible says He is "without sin," and why the Father spoke these words:

"And suddenly a voice *came* from heaven, saying, " This is My beloved Son, *in whom I am well pleased.* "[3]

Jesus lived a sinless life, in absolute harmony with God's goodness, but how many

---

[3] Matthew 3:17

others do? How many people, besides Jesus, will live their whole lives in complete accord with God's wishes? Romans 3:23 gives us the answer.

"For all have sinned and fall short of the glory of God"

According to this verse, *everyone* that has ever lived, with the exception of Jesus, has sinned. At some point in our lives, we have all either done something God wouldn't desire, or *not* done something He would.

For many of us, this truth is not a shocking revelation. We can look back through our mind's eye and point quickly to grave mistakes in our past: things we wish we had never done, or wonderful opportunities now lost to us forever. These memories fill us with regret, and we long for forgiveness and a fresh start.

For others, the idea of being a sinner seems just a little too harsh. You have all certainly made some mistakes, but consider yourselves to be overall good people, and certainly you are. You pay your taxes, give to charities, and treat people kindly. You have most certainly *never* murdered, committed adultery, or been a thief. It seems illogical and severe to group yourselves with all of the evil people who inhabit our world.

Yet the Holy Bible calls every person a *sinner*. How can this be?

The answer lies in a clear understanding of how God views *any* infraction of His righteous will. In a very real way, man's sin has presented God with a *conflict of interest*. God loves us all very deeply- so much so that He would even sacrifice His only son for our salvation.[4] At the same time, God is pulled by an equally strong sense of justice. He is not only the *Father* of mankind, He is also the *Judge*.

> "*He is* the Rock, His work *is* perfect; For all His ways *are* justice, A God of truth and without injustice; Righteous and upright *is* He."[5]

Being the Creator of all things and the very standard of all that is good, God is just in His nature. There is no evil in Him at all. In fact, God is *incapable* of doing wrong, for He is Himself the benchmark that determines what is right.

> "…in hope of eternal life which God, *who cannot lie*, promised before time began."[6]

---

[4] John 3:16
[5] Deuteronomy 32:4
[6] Titus 1:2

You see, regardless of how deeply God loves mankind, and longs to save everyone, He is bound by justice. God *must* do the just thing, regardless of what His love *desires* to do. His nature is absolutely just and good, and He is *limited* and bound by that nature. Therefore, whatever punishment justice demands of sin is that which God must inflict.

"For the wages of sin *is* death..."[7]

According to Romans 6:23, the just punishment of sin is *death*. When we think of death, we always envision a physical death, that is, losing our physical life. However, *death* can mean something else entirely. The word, as it is used in the Bible, often refers to the idea of *separation from God*.

"But of the fruit of the tree which *is* in the midst of the garden, God has said, ' You shall not eat it, nor shall you touch it, *lest you die.* ' "[8]

After Adam and Eve ate of the forbidden fruit, they did not physically die. In fact, Adam lived on to be 800 years old![9] For their

---

[7] Romans 6:23
[8] Genesis 3:3
[9] Genesis 5:4

transgression they were expelled from the Garden of Eden, and hence, from the presence of God. They were separated from Him because of their sin. In this very first story of sin and wrongdoing, we see the pattern of what sin has done in the life of every subsequent sinner, and what it continues to do today. *Sin separates man from God.*

"But your iniquities have separated you from your God; And your sins have hidden *His* face from you, So that He will not hear."[10]

If God's nature is absolutely just, and therefore demands that He impose the just punishment for sin, and if the just punishment for sin is separation from God, is it any wonder that we long to be close to Him again? We were made to be in union with God, but sin has come in the way. It has barred our path back to God, and likewise, barred His path to us.

Nevertheless, God desperately wants to be close to us as well. His love for man is so great that it is almost indescribable. He was willing to pay ANY price to be able to reconcile us to Himself.

---

[10] Isaiah 59:2

Sin has burdened every life. It has alienated us from our God. It has affected my life, and without a doubt, it has affected yours. Read on. The story only gets better as we see the great lengths a loving God will take to win back the children whom He adores!

Step 2

Comprehending God's Love

The separation of man from God is the result of sin. Even though God's justice demanded a fair and right punishment for the sins of mankind, His great love urged Him to create a plan whereby mankind might be saved. Thus, God was faced with the challenge of both punishing every sin AND saving the sinner. How could such utterly conflicting interests ever both be accomplished?

In order to see it done, a *mediator* was needed. A mediator is one who intercedes between two opposing parties to see a conflict resolved. He is a "go between," who equally represents the interests of both and strives to see them reunited. Consider 1 Timothy 2:5:

"For *there is* one God and one Mediator between God and men, *the* Man Christ Jesus"

Imagine a bridge. The bridge spans a wide river and connects both sides. In order for the bridge to be of any use, it MUST touch both shores. In much the same way, our mediator is our *bridge* to God. He spans the gulf of sin and connects mankind to God. He must touch both shores.

I am convinced that this is the reason the Bible is so clear on the nature of Jesus. His deity is made very plain in scripture.

"In the beginning was the Word, and the Word was with God, and the Word was God… And the Word became flesh and dwelt among us, and we beheld His glory, the glory as of the only begotten of the Father, full of grace and truth."[1]

Yet, His humanity is seen in the Word as well.

"Inasmuch then as the children have partaken of flesh and blood, He Himself likewise shared in the same… Therefore, in all things He had to be made like *His* brethren, that He might be a merciful and faithful High Priest in things *pertaining* to God, to make propitiation for the sins of the people."[2]

Jesus, as the mediator between God and man, is both FULLY God and FULLY human. Therefore, He understands and can adequately represent both parties. He is our *bridge* to God, because being both God and man, He *touches both shores*!

---

[1] John 1:1,14
[2] Hebrews 2:14,17

Although Jesus is the perfect mediator, and thereby the *agent* of our reconciliation to God, there still has to be a *means* whereby we can once again approach the Father. Christ is the one by which it is done, but the *gospel* is the way in which He does it.

> "For I am not ashamed of the *gospel of Christ*, for it is *the power of God to salvation* for everyone who believes, for the Jew first and also for the Greek."[3]

The *gospel* was the means by which God determined we could be reunited to Him through Jesus. It is God's power to save us; His solution to the separation caused by sin. Through this *gospel*, God was able to both satisfy His justice AND reconcile sinful man unto Himself.

But, what is the *gospel*? What does this word mean? Most would answer, "It is the Bible," and, in part, they would be right. Every page of the Bible certainly does point us to the gospel, comment on it, and explain it to us; however the gospel is more than simply the words of the Bible.

The word *gospel* basically means, "Good news." What an appropriate definition! What could be better news than that which brings man

---

[3] Romans 1:16

back to God? But Christ has so many beautiful things which are unique to His life and existence: the virgin birth, His earthly ministry, His miracles and healing. What is it about Jesus that God calls *the* good news? Paul gives us the answer in his first letter to the church at Corinth.

> "Moreover, brethren, I declare to you the gospel which I preached to you… that Christ died for our sins according to the Scriptures, and that He was buried, and that He rose again the third day according to the Scriptures"[4]

Although everything about Jesus and His life is certainly *good*, the *gospel* of Jesus is summed up by His death on the cross, burial, and resurrection from the dead. In these lie man's hope to be reunited with God. Through Christ's death and resurrection the Father found a way to both satisfy His justice and show mercy toward those whom He loved.

What a terrible price! In order to pay for man's sin, God had to offer up His own perfect son as a substitute. In essence, God traded His beloved son for us.

To those of us with children, this thought is almost unimaginable! We might give our own life for a noble cause or to save the life of a

---

[4] 1 Corinthians 15:1,3-4

friend, but there is *nothing on earth* that could motivate us to sacrifice the life of a child. There is no cause great enough, no person good enough, and no reason worthy enough for the lives of our children!

The confusion is compounded further when we consider *who* God gave up His Son to save. Mankind was certainly not worthy of such a sacrifice. In fact, many people never even appreciate the enormity of God's love that He would give His only Son.

"For when we were still without strength, in due time Christ died for the ungodly. For scarcely for a righteous man will one die; yet perhaps for a good man someone would even dare to die. But God demonstrates His own love toward us, in that *while we were still sinners*, Christ died for us."[5]

The greatest of gifts was sent to a world which would reject it, to save a people who didn't want or appreciate it, into the hands of a generation who would attempt to destroy it! Isn't it amazing? Could love ever be so great as that of God for mankind?

How can I ever understand such love? Consider Jesus' plea in the Garden of Gethsemane:

---

[5] Romans 5:6-8

17

" My soul is exceedingly sorrowful, even to death. Stay here and watch with Me… O My Father, *if it is possible, let this cup pass from Me*; nevertheless, not as I will, but as You *will.* "[6]

Jesus, in His moment of greatest desperation, is pleading with His Father and asking that God find another path. As I think of Jesus there, afraid and alone, I cannot help but think also of the Father in heaven as He listened to the request. How difficult it must have been to listen to the pleas of His beloved Son and yet still send Him to the pain and suffering of the crucifixion.

When my children cry, when they plead with me, my heart longs to free them from their fear. I am motivated to work with all of my power to make their path less painful and to lighten their load. Wouldn't God have wanted to do the same for Jesus? Can't you imagine the Father as Christ begged Him in the garden to make another way? Were there tears in His eyes? Did He whisper, "I'm sorry Son, but there is no other way?" Because of His love for us, God allowed His only Son to go the way of the cross!

God would watch as His Son was falsely accused, mocked, spat upon, beaten, and

---

[6] Matthew 26:38-39

18

scourged (whipped) almost to death. Then, as Jesus hung on the cross, He cried out:

"And about the ninth hour Jesus cried out with a loud voice, saying, " Eli, Eli, lama sabachthani? " that is, " *My God, My God, why have You forsaken Me?* "[7]

Jesus hung in bitter agony, alone and betrayed, and now, because of *my sin*, even the Father has turned His back on Him. Is there anything that would drag you away from your child's side if he were dying? If he cried out, "Daddy, please don't leave me. I'm in such pain. Please stay with me." Could anything pull you away? As His only Son suffered and approached the moment of His last breath, only one thing was powerful enough to pull the Father away from His side… His love for us!

As we have discussed, death is separation from God. In order for Jesus to be a substitute for our sins, He had to die, not just physically, but spiritually as well. He had to be separated from God. Therefore, as God placed the sins of this world upon His suffering Son, He turned away from that sin, and separated Himself from Jesus.

---

[7] Matthew 27:46

How terrible is our sin? God's Son came to earth, lived a humble life, endured mockery, ridicule, torture, and death, all to pay for our sin. I would say it is pretty terrible! But as horrid as our sin was, consider the love of a God who would send His only Son to take our place! I will never fully comprehend such love, but one thing I do know- my God *really loves me*, and *He loves you the same*!!!

Step 3

Choosing Our Road

We all appreciate choices. We like extensive menus with a wide variety of foods, and huge car lots with every make and color. Making our own decisions is a hallmark of our American independence, and considered the ultimate benefit of finally achieving adulthood. When it comes to the question of building a relationship with God, life again comes down to a decision. God's love in sending Jesus has presented us with a choice.

God has always wanted mankind to have choices. We often call this *free-will.*

> *"Choose for yourselves* this day whom you will serve, whether the gods which your fathers served... But as for me and my house, we will serve the LORD. "[1]

Couldn't God force us to do the right thing? If He is all powerful, wouldn't He be able to demand that we love Him? Most certainly He could. But would it be love? If you are forced to say "I love you," is there any

---

[1] Joshua 24:15

emotion or real affection behind it? If a robot was programmed to tell you "I love you," would you ever feel truly loved? Without a choice made of one's free-will, there is no love, only service.

" And now, Israel, what does the LORD your God require of you, but to fear the LORD your God, to walk in all His ways and to love Him, to serve the LORD your God with all your heart and with all your soul, and to keep the commandments of the LORD and His statutes which I command you today for your good?"[2]

God's desire is that we love Him, but in order for us to do so, we must choose Him over the alternative. It was true with Adam and Eve as they made the choice to eat the forbidden fruit rather than obey God, and the choice remains the same today. We can decide to go our own way, living in sin, or we can choose the Lord's way, and accept what God and Christ have done for us through the cross.

" Enter by the narrow gate; for wide *is* the gate and broad *is* the way that leads to destruction, and there are many who go in by it. Because narrow *is* the gate and difficult *is* the way which leads to life, and there are few who find it."[3]

---

[2] Deuteronomy 10:12-13
[3] Matthew 7:13-14

It isn't that the Father desires that anyone be lost, or choose the wide road to destruction. On the contrary, the Bible is clear that God loves all people and desperately desires their salvation. Isn't the gospel of Christ's death, burial, and resurrection proof of that?

"The Lord is not slack concerning *His* promise, as some count slackness, but is longsuffering toward us, *not willing that any should perish* but that all should come to repentance."[4]

Although God desperately desires that we repent and live for Him, and thereby be saved, He isn't going to force anyone. The decision still rests in the hands of every individual. This choice is the essence of belief and faith, whereby man decides to accept Christ's gift and follow His will.

"And if anyone hears My words and does not believe, I do not judge him; for I did not come to judge the world but to save the world. He who rejects Me, and does not receive My words, has that which judges him— the word that I have spoken will judge him in the last day."[5]

This is the essence of our choice: to either believe in Christ and obey Him, or reject Him and follow our own path. To believe in Him is

---

[4] 2 Peter 3:9
[5] John 12:47-48

to acknowledge Him as Lord and Master of our lives. There can be only one master. Each of us has a "throne" which determines our course and direction, and there is only room for one person to be seated there… either Christ or me. I cannot have it both ways.

> " No one can serve two masters; for either he will hate the one and love the other, or else he will be loyal to the one and despise the other…"[6]

In the context of Matthew 6:24, the two masters are God and money, but the application is clear… everyone must make a choice. There can only be one master of my life. Will I continue to direct my own steps and live in my own desires, apart from God? Or do I choose another path? Will I willingly choose Christ by believing that He is the Son of God who died on the cross for my sins, and will I make Him absolute Master of my life by obeying His commands?

Your answer will determine if you read on, and thereby draw close to God. What will your choice be? Who will you place on the throne of your life?

---

[6] Matthew 6:24

Step 4

Looking Toward A New Beginning

What would a person give to be able to go back in time and do things over? If mistakes and regrets could be "re-done," who wouldn't take the opportunity? We all have "dark ages" in our pasts- times we wish we could take back and long to forget.

However, this cannot be done. Life doesn't have a "reset" button. Time marches forward, and the past becomes unreachable and unchangeable. The things we wish we hadn't done are always there, at the edge of our memories, and nothing we can do can make them "not have been." Or, are they?

What if we could have our *record expunged*? Simply put, it would mean that the guilt of our past would no longer be counted against us. In essence, we would have a clean slate; and be, for all practical purposes, innocent and guiltless.

Yes, there would still be the memories of our past. When a guilty criminal has his record wiped clean, he still remembers the deeds he has done, and it would be the same for us. We would then be able to move forward, knowing that the indiscretions of our youth are behind us, and that we have been given a second chance at life. What a beautiful dream!

It is more than just a fanciful and unrealistic notion. Although the man on death row may hope for the pardon which will never come, our pardon has already been issued!

"Now to Him who is able to keep you from stumbling, and to present *you faultless* before the presence of His glory with exceeding joy"[1]

Christ is able to present us as *faultless* before God, the Judge of all mankind. Because of Jesus, we can be perfect, without blemish, and guiltless in the eyes of the Father.

It is therefore no wonder that Christ Jesus calls the salvation process a *new birth*.

"Jesus answered and said to him, " Most assuredly, I say to you, unless one is born again, he cannot see the kingdom of God. "[2]

Imagine the concept of being *born again*. It fills us with hope of a new beginning. It whispers of a life where all of our mistakes were

---

[1] Jude 24
[2] John 3:3

never committed, and in which we have nothing but good things to look forward to. It truly is a dream come true: being able to do it all over again. Could there be a more beautiful image of hope?

"Therefore, if anyone *is* in Christ, *he is* a new creation; old things have passed away; behold, all things have become new."[3]

How is a person to be "born again?" The question is not new. Even Nicodemus, the very person who first heard Christ's teaching on the subject, was confused by it. The seeming absurdity of the concept baffled him.

"Nicodemus said to Him, " How can a man be born when he is old? Can he enter a second time into his mother's womb and be born? "[4]

The question is an absurd sounding response to an absurd sounding command. Once a person is born, he grows older, until finally death takes him. That is the way of the world. People are only born once. So how can a man be "born again?" How can we hit the "reset button," and start over? Jesus answers our questions in His response to Nicodemus.

---

[3] 2 Corinthians 5:17
[4] John 3:4

"… Most assuredly, I say to you, unless one is born of water and the Spirit, he cannot enter the kingdom of God. That which is born of the flesh is flesh, and that which is born of the Spirit is spirit."[5]

Whereas the first birth is physical, the *new birth* is spiritual. It is an inner change which God works in a person's life. When someone responds to Christ's gift of salvation through obedience, God re-creates his inner being, making him once again pure and innocent like a newborn baby.

Jesus connects this new birth to both water and spirit, and in these two things we begin to understand what He was saying. The *water* is very significant. Jesus is referring to the act of obedience known as *baptism*. Baptism is so much more than simply a ceremonial act of washing. It is a moment of change. At the point of our baptism we see the culmination of what the Bible calls "faith," and the miracle of salvation takes place in our lives.

How does this occur? What is so significant about this act which seems so commonplace? To answer, we must first realize that it is a work of God and not a work of man. Baptism is something to which we *submit*

---

[5] John 3:5-6

28

ourselves, not something we *do ourselves*. This is an important distinction, because there is nothing we can *do* in order to earn our salvation. Works cannot cause anyone to be saved.

"For by grace you have been saved through faith, and that not of yourselves; *it is* the gift of God, not of works, lest anyone should boast."[6]

What is it then that God does for us through baptism? We know that His saving power is wrapped up in Christ's awesome sacrifice on the cross and His glorious resurrection. But how do we connect with that sacrifice? How do we become united to the salvation brought through Jesus' death and resurrection? Pay close attention to Paul's explanation in Romans 6.

"Or do you not know that as many of us as were baptized into Christ Jesus were baptized into His death? Therefore we were buried with Him through baptism into death, that just as Christ was raised from the dead by the glory of the Father, even so we also should walk in newness of life. For if we have been united together in the likeness of His death, certainly we also shall be *in the likeness* of *His* resurrection, knowing this, that *our old man was crucified with Him,* that the body of sin might be done away with, that we should no longer be slaves of sin."[7]

---

[6] Ephesians 2:8-9
[7] Romans 6:3-6

Paul describes the old person as *dying*, and a new person being brought forth at the moment of baptism. It is here where we touch the saving power of Christ's sacrifice on the cross. In our baptism we submit ourselves wholly to God's will, and in that moment His divine grace strips away all of our guilt, and credits us with the righteousness of Jesus Christ.

In this way we become *new*, hence the distinction of being *born again*. When God looks at the life of a born again believer, He no longer sees a life of sin, for that sin has been washed away. Instead, He sees a perfect and pure life like that of a newborn baby. This puts Christ's statements about becoming as "little children" in perspective, showing us that we can, through the process of new birth, be innocent and pure again.

> "Then Jesus called a little child to Him, set him in the midst of them, and said, 'Assuredly, I say to you, *unless you are converted and become as little children*, you will by no means enter the kingdom of heaven.'"[8]

What a glorious message to those who have been burdened by guilt: they can be pure again! It is possible, through faith and the new

---

[8] Matthew 18:2-3

birth, to be an innocent again in the sight of God!

Can a person go back in time and start over? Through the blood of Jesus, faith, and the new birth it can be accomplished in the way that matters most… in the eyes of God the Judge!

Step 5

Living A New Life

For most of us, the idea of starting over with a *clean slate* is vastly appealing. Guilt has burdened our lives and caused us to feel spiritually dirty and inadequate, making the idea of being innocent in God's sight glorious indeed. Yet there often remains one lingering question, "What about *after* I am cleansed of my sins?"

We know ourselves. We have weaknesses, and they seem to always sneak up on us even when we think we have them beat. We try our best, but yet we fall. As we look at the cleansing power of new birth, we again face the agonizing truth of guilt; not the guilt of what we *have* done, but the realization of what we *will* do! There can be no denying that although God has said He will cleanse us through Christ, we will *someday sin again*, and every one of us knows it!

"If we say that we have no sin, we deceive ourselves, and the truth is not in us… If we say that we have not sinned, we make Him a liar, and His word is not in us."[1]

---

[1] 1 John 1:8,10

John was addressing Christians. In chapter 2, verse 7, he refers to his readers as "Brethren." This tells us that people who have been born again, for all Christians have, are still tempted and commit sin. Therefore, we ask the inevitable question, "What happens after my sins have been washed away and then I sin again?"

The first thing to realize is that, although we will still make mistakes, we have resources in Christ we did not have before. For one thing, we have the Holy Spirit living within us.

"Then Peter said to them, " Repent, and let every one of you be baptized in the name of Jesus Christ for the remission of sins; *and you shall receive the gift of the Holy Spirit.* "[2]

"Likewise *the Spirit also helps in our weaknesses.* For we do not know what we should pray for as we ought, but the Spirit Himself makes intercession for us with groanings which cannot be uttered."[3]

The Bible tells us that as born-again people, we have become *temples* of the Holy Spirit.[4] Consider what this means. God's presence has taken up residency within us, and He is with us at every moment. What greater resource could we have? What could possibly

---

[2] Acts 2:38
[3] Romans 8:26
[4] 1 Corinthians 6:19

help us more as we endeavor to resist temptation and live holy lives?

"But the *fruit of the Spirit* is love, joy, peace, longsuffering, kindness, goodness, faithfulness, gentleness, self-control. Against such there is no law."[5]

The Spirit produces wonderful fruit in our lives and helps us as we strive to live right and refrain from sinning. What a marvelous encouragement. We have God with us all the time to help us when we need Him! Will this remove temptation from our lives? Certainly not. In fact, Satan may "turn up the heat," but it will give us the ability to resist if we will choose to.

"No temptation has overtaken you except such as is common to man; but God *is* faithful, who will not allow you to be tempted beyond what you are able, but with the temptation will also make the way of escape, that you may be able to bear *it*."[6]

No temptation will ever come our way that we cannot resist. We have been given, through the Holy Spirit, the power to escape any enticement, no matter how difficult. What greater resource could there be for the born-again believer?

---

[5] Galatians 5:22-23
[6] 1 Corinthians 10:13

We will make mistakes and we will sometimes fail. The important thing is that we constantly strive to be godly and righteous. All of us who are parents understand this principle. We see our kids as they make an effort at baseball or soccer, and sometimes they fail and fall down. Then comes the moment of decision, when our parental feelings are directed down either the path of pride or disappointment. The child who gets up and tries again brings us a sense of pride, but the one who pouts and quits disappoints us. We want them to *try* and give it their best and so does God. What matters to Him is that, although we sometimes fall, we get up and walk the road of righteousness again.

But if we walk in the light as He is in the light, we have fellowship with one another, and the blood of Jesus Christ His Son cleanses us from all sin.[7]

God's expectation of those who have been born again is not *perfection*, but *direction*. None of us will ever be perfect in this life, and God doesn't expect us to be. He is interested in our effort. He wants us to try our very best to attain righteousness, and when we occasionally fall, to get up and try again. This process is described

---

[7] 1 John 1:7

as *walking in the light,* and shows us that, although we may stumble along the way, God is concerned with us getting up and continuing the walk.

The blessing for this continuous effort is glorious: He *cleanses us from all sin.* What an encouragement! Although I know I will make mistakes, and God knows I will make mistakes, my sins will continuously be cleansed as long as I am *trying* to live for Him and acknowledge how much I need Him. Therefore I can be confident, because with God, the words of every little league coach prove to be an eternal truth: *It's the effort that counts*! Is it any wonder that John will discuss the absolute confidence of a believer who is walking in the light?

These things I have written to you who believe in the name of the Son of God, that you may know that you have eternal life, and that you may *continue to* believe in the name of the Son of God.[8]

There is a second possibility included in the John 1:7. It is *walking in darkness.* This tells us that although salvation is clearly achievable through daily striving, it is not an unconditional guarantee. Just as we can be

---

[8] 1 John 5:13

assured of our salvation through the effort of walking in the light, we can equally be assured of being lost if we turn to walk in darkness. Therefore, how we live day to day definitely matters. Our lifestyle dictates our direction. If we turn away from God, live in wickedness, and pursue darkness, the blood no longer covers our sin and we become lost.

> For if we sin willfully after we have received the knowledge of the truth, there no longer remains a sacrifice for sins, but a certain fearful expectation of judgment, and fiery indignation which will devour the adversaries.[9]

You won't be perfect, in fact you can't be perfect, but you can try! Isn't it wonderful that your best effort is all that God expects? With this standard we can have absolute confidence that once we are born again, salvation can indeed be ours until the day we die!

---

[9] Hebrews 10:26-27

Step 6

Drawing Close Every Day

What is essential for any healthy relationship?

Although this question may seem like the cliché investigation of some television psychologist, the pop-culture answer is indeed both correct and necessary. Sometimes Dr. Phil gets it right. Healthy relationships require *communication*.

My profession has taken me many different places throughout my life. I have lived in the Northwest, the West, the Southwest, and even the Deep South. In each of these places I have made dear friends that were very special to me. Yet today there are only a select few that I remain *close to*. How do I know? What is the criteria whereby I determine who has remained a *close* friend and who hasn't? The difference is that there are some I have kept in contact with and others whom I have not.

Contact is the key to communication. In order to have a relationship, we have to have some level of interaction. We have to *talk* to one another. What is a marriage if a husband and wife never talk? What relationship do parents have with their children if they never speak? They have very little, and if it isn't corrected, they will soon have none at all.

So it is in our relationship with God. He has paid the price through Jesus and brought us near, but how do we stay that way? How do we keep that closeness without drifting back into our old ways and waking up one day to realize we are again far away from God? We keep communication with Him through two means: *prayer* and *study*.

Prayer is the means whereby we communicate to God.

> Be anxious for nothing, but in everything by prayer and supplication, with thanksgiving, let your requests be made known to God.[1]

Prayer is really little more than talking with God. In our prayers we can express joy or pain, excitement or fear, and even love or anger. It is a conversation with God, who is our Father, and should show Him our true hearts, revealing all of our deep emotions and thoughts.

---

[1] Philippians 4:6

Then Jesus came with them to a place called Gethsemane, and said to the disciples, "Sit here while I go and pray over there." And He took with Him Peter and the two sons of Zebedee, and He began to be sorrowful and deeply distressed. Then He said to them, "My soul is exceedingly sorrowful, even to death. Stay here and watch with Me." He went a little farther and fell on His face, and prayed, saying, "O My Father, if it is possible, let this cup pass from Me; nevertheless, not as I will, but as You *will.*"[2]

In these verses Jesus is very deeply disturbed, knowing that His death is coming. What does He do in response? He prays. He goes off alone and, in tears, tells God about the problem. God is His Father and His Friend, just like He is to us, and Jesus longs to share His most intimate thoughts and fears with Him.

Pray without ceasing, in everything give thanks; for this is the will of God in Christ Jesus for you.[3]

Jesus was constantly in communication with God, talking with Him through prayer. We must do the same. God wants us to share everything with Him - our very lives. He wants us to tell Him about our joys, our hurts, our triumphs, and our defeats. What else would we expect from a loving father and friend?

---

[2] Matthew 26:36-39
[3] 1 Thessalonians 5:17-18

40

Communication cannot flow only one way. God also desires to communicate with us. How exactly does God speak to you and me? Does He talk directly with us? Most of us (a few notwithstanding) would quickly recognize that He does not. We don't hear little voices from God. Does He communicate through our feelings? Likewise, we all know that emotions can be very confusing and even deceptive at times, so how does God speak to us?

"I do not pray for these alone, but also for those who will believe in Me through their word; that they all may be one, as You, Father, *are* in Me, and I in You; that they also may be one in Us, that the world may believe that You sent Me.[4]

Jesus, while praying for His Apostles, also prays for a second group: those who would believe in Him through the words of those Apostles. In this, He prays for all of us. You and I have developed all of our faiths because of what we read in the Bible, which was written down for us by the Apostles.

...knowing this first, that no prophecy of Scripture is of any private interpretation, for prophecy never came by the will of

---

[4] John 17:20-21

man, but holy men of God spoke *as they were* moved by the Holy Spirit.[5]

If anyone thinks himself to be a prophet or spiritual, let him acknowledge that the things which I write to you are the commandments of the Lord.[6]

The words we read in the Bible are not just the thoughts and opinions of the Apostles. They are the words given to them by God for us. The Bible is the means by which God has chosen to communicate His will to us. It is how He instructs and rebukes us; it is how He commands and informs us. In short, the Bible is how God *talks* to us.

Be diligent to present yourself approved to God, a worker who does not need to be ashamed, rightly dividing the word of truth.[7]

In this verse, Paul instructs Timothy in how to best utilize God's Word by telling him to "be diligent." The King James translates this as, "*Study* to show yourself approved." Young Timothy is advised to be very serious about his Bible study, working with a very deliberate purpose.

---

[5] 2 Peter 1:20-21
[6] 1 Corinthians 14:37
[7] 2 Timothy 2:15

Consider with me the possibilities this opens up for us. The Bible is the most marvelous book ever written. The wisdom of the Creator of heaven and earth is contained in its pages, and has been given to us for our learning. It contains the very words of God and instructions for how to handle any situation that life will throw our way. In a very real sense, it is a manual for life: an answer book for all the questions of living.

All Scripture *is* given by inspiration of God, and *is* profitable for doctrine, for reproof, for correction, for instruction in righteousness, *that the man of God may be complete, thoroughly equipped for every good work.*[8]

Knowing this, wouldn't anyone want to make Bible study part of his or her regular routine?

Relationships cannot exist without communication. Any marriage, partnership, family, or friendship is eventually doomed without it, so it is with our relationship to God. Thankfully, He has given us a viable and rewarding means of communication: prayer and Bible study. Please pray to God every day. Begin your day with prayer. Pray in your car, in the shower, at work, before your meals…

---

[8] 2 Timothy 3:16-17

whenever you get a moment. He wants to hear from you often and regularly. Then, let God speak to you. Get into the routine of studying your Bible every day. Make the time. It might just be a chapter or two at a time, but the rewards will be endless. He wants relationship; He has put forth all the effort. He wants to hear from you and to speak to you in return!

Step 7

Being Faithful

There can be nothing more important in any relationship than *faithfulness*. It is the test of true devotion and love. It is the virtue that authenticates the bond and communicates an intention to "stick with" one another to the end. We value faithful friends, family members, and especially spouses as the people in life on whom we can truly depend.

In fact, we have little use for the unfaithful. No one wants a "fair-weather friend" or a spouse who is not true. Every employer wants employees who keep their word and show up for work. Unfaithfulness is the essence of being undependable. Such people are never there when you *really* need them. In short, they always let you down.

Why would it be any different with God? We have seen His abundant love; is it any wonder that He desires *faithful love* from us in return?

Therefore whoever confesses Me before men, him I will also confess before My Father who is in heaven. But whoever denies

Me before men, him I will also deny before My Father who is in heaven.[1]

Jesus' statement reveals His attitude toward those who claim to love Him yet reveal themselves as unfaithful. He will reject them on the final day. The promise of faithfulness toward us on the part of Christ at judgment day is *dependant* on our faithfulness toward Him as we live out our lives. At the point of our baptism, we make a commitment to Christ, and He expects us to remain true to that commitment.

Faithfulness is expressed in a number of ways. We know God doesn't demand perfection but simply a faithful effort to live for Him. So what exactly should we do? What does a faithful life look like?

First of all, it avoids worldly things.

Adulterers and adulteresses! Do you not know that friendship with the world is enmity with God? Whoever therefore wants to be a friend of the world makes himself an enemy of God. Or do you think that the Scripture says in vain, "The Spirit who dwells in us yearns jealously"?[2]

---

[1] Matthew 10:32-33
[2] James 4:4-5

We understand jealousy. If someone we love "flirts" with another, it causes us to be angry. What if the "flirting" is with your arch-enemy? The same is true with God. When Christians enjoy the wicked things of the world, what does that say to our God? He is jealous, and it causes Him to be angry.

This doesn't mean that we have to quit our jobs, lock ourselves up in a commune, and cease all contact with people outside of Christ. In fact, God wants us to reach the lost and bring them into our Christian family.[3] What God doesn't want is for us to get *too* close to worldly people. We must limit the scope of our relationships and always be on guard that we are being an influence on *them*, and not the other way around.

Perhaps this is why God is so concerned that His people be involved with *the Church*. When we were saved (baptized into Christ), the Bible teaches that God added us to His church.

...praising God and having favor with all the people. And the Lord added to the church daily those who were being saved.[4]

---

[3] Mark 16:15-16
[4] Acts 2:47

From that moment we were made a part of a community of like-minded people. We became one with all the saved throughout the world. This group of every saved person is simply called *the Church*.

As His Church (a community of saved people) God intends for us to be a support for one another to help each other deal with temptation, suffering, and persecution. Speaking to first century Christians, Peter instructed them:

And above all things have fervent love for one another, for *"love will cover a multitude of sins." Be* hospitable to one another without grumbling. As each one has received a gift, minister it to one another, as good stewards of the manifold grace of God.[5]

The Church is a family. As Satan attacks us and tempts us at every turn, God intends that we lean upon one another for strength and comfort. To do so, we have to be in constant contact with each other. If a Christian is all alone in a hostile world, how long will he make it before giving up his faith and yielding to temptation? This is why church attendance is so important, not simply to fulfill a requirement, but to put believers in contact with one another

---

[5] 1 Peter 4:8-10

so that they can help each other to resist the world.

> And let us consider one another in order to stir up love and good works, not forsaking the assembling of ourselves together, as *is* the manner of some, but exhorting *one another,* and so much the more as you see the Day approaching.[6]

You see, our relationship with God goes hand in hand with our relationship in the Church. Because the moment of our salvation and the moment we were added to the Church are the same (Acts 2:47), we see that a person cannot be saved apart from being in the Church. The two are one and the same. Therefore, every believer must be an active part of a local congregation of the Church to remain faithful in relationship with Christ.

Can you image a spouse who said he was committed but never came home? How about a "committed" employee who never showed up for work? Commitment requires an active presence. We must be present in the Church of God to be in community with Him.

This can be one of the hardest aspects of Christianity, especially at first. Regular church

------

[6] Hebrews 10:24-25

attendance requires discipline and motivation. Satan will always make our schedules busy and tempt us with other things to do. He wants us to find every excuse to put off church and prioritize other things. In time, duty will become habit, and attendance will become easier. Until that time comes, a Christian must commit himself to be a faithful attender, and make every effort to arrange his schedule so that he can attend as many services and activities of the Church as possible.

Step 8

Which Church Do I Choose?

In many ways this is a difficult chapter to write. The truth is that there are over 300 different churches in America today, and all of them believe and practice somewhat different things. Any sincere person worshipping in any of those religious groups would naturally encourage you to choose their particular one. This is only natural considering that *they* chose it and obviously thought it to be better than the rest for some reasons. Those reasons might involve any number of factors including family traditions, cultural preferences, or doctrinal preconceptions.

The problem is that such an encouragement can sound arrogant. It can come across that "my church is the best church," which has a tone of discrimination and elitism. This is the dilemma we find ourselves in at this point. How do we encourage one church over another without seeming haughty or condescending?

It would be easier if it didn't matter. If all the churches were fundamentally the same, it wouldn't make any difference and the only decision to make would be one of taste and preference. However, all churches are *not* the same. In truth, they vary greatly in their worship, doctrines, and attitudes. But does that matter? Do the details really make any difference? If they didn't, wouldn't all the things we've learned in this book so far be inconsequential? If the Bible isn't intended to be followed and obeyed, then does anything we do or not do matter anyway?

The fact is that when it comes to Churches, you really can't judge a book by its cover. Some claim to be Christian, but don't even believe Jesus is really God (we've studied how important that is). Some teach salvation, but never mention being born again. You can't always tell these things from worshipping with people or simply having casual conversation. It is going to take some *biblical investigation* for you to find a Church where you can live a Christian life pleasing to God.

I'm not going to tell you which church to attend, but I will give you some suggestions of how to identify a *Biblical* Church (one that is following the Bible's instructions about what the church should be).

1. *What is the church's focus?* Church should be all about worshipping God, but many times we make it about us. When asked why they worship a particular place, people will often answer, "Because I like the _____!" This indicates a completely backwards focus. We attend church to please God, not to please ourselves.

The best way to determine a church's focus is to ask the question "why?" Sit down with the preacher or leaders and ask them about their practices, their worship, and their services. If the answers given involve "we think it will reach more people," or "that's what today's generation wants," be very leery. Reaching the lost is a wonderful objective, but there is a very fine line between being adaptable and compromising God's will. Whenever a church totally focuses on "what works," or "what brings in the most people," they have forgotten that church is all about God, *not* all about us!

2. *What does the church teach about salvation?* As we studied new birth (chapter 4), the need for baptism was seen again and again. According to the scriptures, baptism is a vital part of the salvation process.

And now why are you waiting? Arise and *be baptized, and wash away your sins,* calling on the name of the Lord.'[1]

There is also an antitype *which now saves us—baptism* (not the removal of the filth of the flesh, but the answer of a good conscience toward God), through the resurrection of Jesus Christ[2]

These verses, along with those we studied in chapter 4, show us that being baptized is the last stage of the process of saving faith. It is *the moment* our sins are forgiven and we are added to the kingdom of God's people. Yet many churches do not teach this. They often ignore the need for baptism all together, or de-emphasize its importance by saying it is simply an act of obedience *after* a person is already saved. But how could that be true?

Then Peter said to them, "Repent, and let every one of you *be baptized in the name of Jesus Christ for the remission of sins*; and you shall receive the gift of the Holy Spirit.[3]

The people on Pentecost were told that baptism was *for* the remission (forgiveness) of sins. It was not an afterthought or an optional obedience to be put off until it was conveinient. It was *essential* to the salvation process.

---

[1] Acts 22:16
[2] 1 Peter 3:21
[3] Acts 2:38

As you search for a church, this is a very important belief to ask about. Some churches may seem to think baptism is important, and may even do a lot of baptizing, but still think of baptism as simply an option. The difference is between the words "important" and "essential." The best way to find out is simply to ask a leader, "Can a person be saved *without* being baptized?" If he answers "yes," you definitely want to keep searching.

3. *What kind of leadership does the church have?* This criteria is very easy to apply, because the first people you encounter in a church will be in some form of leadership. In this area, there is a great deal of diversity. Different churches have pastors, preachers, ministers, bishops, priests, deacons, lay-people, elders, choir directors, youth ministers, and some even have alter boys. What form of leadership does the Bible describe for the Church? How does Jesus want His Church organized? The following scriptures show us:

For this reason I left you in Crete, that you should set in order the things that are lacking, and *appoint elders* in every city as I commanded you.[4]
Likewise *the deacons* must be reverent...[5]

---

[4] Titus 1:5
[5] 1 Timothy 3:8

And He Himself gave some to be apostles, some prophets, some evangelists, and some pastors and teachers.[6]

The New Testament speaks of Apostles, Prophets, Elders (also called Bishops in some translations), Evangelists (who we sometimes call preachers or ministers), and Deacons. The Apostles were the original twelve men who followed Christ and penned most of the New Testament for us (including Paul), just as the Prophets gave us much of the Old Testament. The scriptures tell us that they were inspired of God.[7] They continue to teach us today every time we open and read the Bible. Yet there are no apostles in this day and time. The qualifications for apostleship (having been with Jesus and seen Him in the flesh after His resurrection[8]) could not be achieved by anyone living today.

That leaves us with three positions of leadership mentioned in scripture that are still in existence today: Elders (or Bishops), Evangelists (or Preachers), and Deacons. The Elders are to lead the church according to the desires of Christ, while the Evangelist preaches to

---

[6] Ephesians 4:11
[7] 1 Corinthians 14:37 and 2 Peter 1:20-21
[8] Acts 1:15-26

encourage and rebuke the members[9], and the Deacons serve. Therefore, we can look at how a church is led and see if they are trying to follow the scriptures. Do they have an eldership? Does the preacher have total control or does he defer to the judgment of the elders? Are the deacons decision makers or do they simply serve? All of these questions will help when trying to find a church like the one in the Bible.

    4. Does the church worship like the church in the Bible? The absolute first thing we can determine about a church is concerning worship. All we have to do is attend services and it is evident. The church we read about in the Bible did certain things in their worship. Some examples of these are:

> And they continued steadfastly in the Apostles' doctrine and fellowship, in the *breaking of bread*, and in *prayers*.[10]

> On the first day of the week let each one of you lay *something aside*, storing up as he may prosper…[11]

> Now on the first day of the week, when the disciples came together *to break bread*, Paul, ready to depart the next day, *spoke to them*…[12]

---

[9] 2 Timothy 4:1-5
[10] Acts 2:42
[11] 1 Corinthians 16:2
[12] Acts 20:7

…Be filled with the Spirit, speaking to one another in psalms, hymns, and spiritual songs, singing and making melody in your heart to the Lord.[13]

In these passages we see that the first Christians prayed, gave according to their means, took communion, preached, and sang songs to God. If a church is trying to be the Church of the Bible, wouldn't all of these practices be present in their assemblies? We can see how much a church values the instructions of scripture just by observing *what they do* as they worship.

All of these criteria are helpful when finding a church, but none of them are comprehensive. There are many more qualities found in scripture by which a church can, and should, be measured. With the Word of God as a guide and measuring stick, I truly believe that a person can find a church similar to the original one we read of in the Bible, and please God by worshipping there.

With all of this in mind, let me humbly recommend to you the churches of Christ. Although not every congregation that goes by the name *Church of Christ* would fit these biblical criteria, and you still will have to do

---

[13] Ephesians 5:18-19

some examination in order to determine if you should worship with a particular one, many of them are very biblical.

Generally, churches of Christ teach that baptism is essential in the saving process, have a desire to put God first, are led by a biblical leadership of elders, and are trying to worship like they original church did. We even go so far as to sing acappella, because we only see singing without instrumental accompaniment in the New Testament. Our worship is thereby rather simple, without much fanfare. It is designed to put God first and please Him.

You now know how to draw closer to God. It isn't quite as hard as it seems, is it? God made the initiative; He loved us first. Now the "ball is in your court" as to what you'll do with it. Do you want to draw close to God? Then what are you waiting for?

CPSIA information can be obtained
at www.ICGtesting.com
Printed in the USA
FFHW021803240819
54457608-60147FF